Stories

for YOU

RICKY KENNISON

AuthorHouse™
1663 Liberty Drive
Bloomington, IN 47403
www.authorhouse.com
Phone: 1 (800) 839-8640

Because of the dynamic nature of the Internet, any web addresses or links contained in this book may have changed
since publication and may no longer be valid. The views expressed in this work are solely those of the author and do not
necessarily reflect the views of the publisher, and the publisher hereby disclaims any responsibility for them.

Any people depicted in stock imagery provided by Getty Images are models,
and such images are being used for illustrative purposes only.
Certain stock imagery © Getty Images.

This book is printed on acid-free paper.

ISBN: 978-1-7283-2304-6(sc)
ISBN: 978-1-7283-2303-9(e)

Library of Congress Control Number: 2019911730

Print information available on the last page.

Published by AuthorHouse 08/14/2019

authorHOUSE®

Contents

A WISH FOR YOU:
A First-Grader's Story from 1957

The year was 1957, and I was beginning my first year in school—first grade—at North Kansas City Elementary school in Missouri.

There was no lunchroom. At lunchtime, a server pushed a lunch cart, stopping at each room with plates and hot food. We formed lines at the door of our classroom. The server put food on the plates and then handed them to us. There were no choices of what to take from the cart to eat. We got whatever was on the pushcart.

Early in the morning, we lined up by the sink in the back of the classroom. Mrs. Earlee gave each of us a vitamin tablet and a paper cup of water at the sink. We then returned to our seats at our desks. There was no breakfast served, just vitamins and lunch.

Mrs. Earlee would have us do projects. One day she told us about the weather. After that, each morning we took turns going to the classroom window and looking out, reporting to the class if it was partly cloudy or partly sunny, or just sunny.

My room was right inside the entrance doors to the school. It was the first room. The school was on one level; there was no upstairs or downstairs. Next to the school was a public park.

Down the street from the school was a public library. Since the school had no library, Mrs. Earlee took us to the public library to get books. We would form a single line inside the classroom. She walked us in single file the almost four blocks to the public library. Inside the library, we looked for books to take with us to read. After we all selecting our books, Mrs. Earlee walked us back down the sidewalk to the school and our classroom.

One day, Mrs. Earlee decided to take us to the public park next to the school. We lined up like we did for the library and walked to the public park next to the school. She gathered us all around her. Mrs. Earlee told us she was going to have a contest with a prize for the winner. It's been a long time since 1957, and I cannot remember the prize she had for us. But I remember we were all excited to win. Mrs. Earlee had a box of saltine crackers and she said, "The contest goes like this." Everyone was to eat one cracker when she said go. The first student who could whistle would win the prize. We were all excited, jumping and moving around to get a saltine cracker.

One girl told me she couldn't whistle and asked me to whistle for her. My reaction was to tell her I was going to whistle for myself. The little girl asked the little boy standing next to us if he would whistle for her because she couldn't whistle. I didn't hear the little boy's answer.

Mrs. Earlee told us all to get ready to eat the cracker, and then she said go. We all put the crackers in our mouths and began chewing. Somehow, the little girl who couldn't whistle finished first. She again asked me to whistle for her. I tried to whistle, but my mouth was too dry from eating the cracker. The little girl saw I couldn't whistle, so she asked the other little boy she asked earlier to whistle for her.

He whistled. Mrs. Earlee was excited. But when she told him he was the winner, the little boy replied that the little girl had finished first but couldn't whistle. He was whistling for her. What a surprise for all of us!

I have always wished it was me who whistled for the little girl who couldn't whistle, even though I couldn't whistle at that time either.

My wish for you is to be the one who whistles for the little girl who can't.

GRANDMOTHER EMMA'S SECRET RECIPE:
Loving and Caring

Grandmother's secret recipe, oh, so good. Grandmother always gave a lot of loving and caring. She always made me feel special. Grandmother lived with Grandfather in a little house next to the Missouri River.

There was a man-made levee between her house and the river. A man used to cut the grass on the levee on her side of the levee. Horses pulled the rolling knives that cut the grass. I was small, and I liked to watch the horses cut the grass.

There were bridges crossing the Missouri River on both sides of Grandmother's house. On the top side of the bridges, cars crossed; on the underside of the bridge, trains crossed the river. My uncle Everett, my grandmother's oldest son, would take me across the levee to fish in the river. We sometimes even caught some, and it was a lot of fun.

In the backyard at Grandmother's house was a pump for pumping water out of the ground. She had water in the house by then but still used the pump sometimes. The pump was painted red.

From time to time, homeless men traveled past the back of Grandmother's house along the levee between the bridges. Back then, these men were called hobos, and they rode the rails, hopping trains to travel from place to place. Many times they stopped by Grandmother's house and said they were hungry or thirsty. Grandmother told me to pump water from the well so they could have a drink, and she fixed something for them to eat. She usually had a roll of bologna she sliced herself. The bologna was often sliced unevenly when she made the sandwiches. The slices were usually thick on one edge and thin on the other.

The homeless men were always so thankful to Grandmother. They smiled and waved as they walked away toward the bridges. If the homeless men asked for another bologna sandwich, she always gave them one. Grandfather said the homeless men would place a mark somewhere for the others to see. It showed the others where they could get something to eat. I guess Grandfather knew because a lot of homeless men stopped and said they were hungry. Of course, Grandmother gave them each a bologna sandwich and a tin glass of water from that red pump.

Grandmother has been gone for a long time now, but her secret recipe, loving and caring, lives on.

Try Grandmother's secret recipe sometimes. It's a lot of fun!

WASP ON THE CEILING

Mr. Wasp, what are doing on the kitchen ceiling? You are supposed to be outside, in your own house. I see you there, Mr. Wasp, as I lay back in my easy chair by the kitchen table. Seems like you don't know where you are. I see your house by the garage door when I drive the care inside. You must have come into the garage when the garage door opened for the car. Then inside the house you came when the door from the garage to house was opened. Now you're looking for a way outside. You're not going to be able to open the door to go out on your own.

I could get some spray and spray you. I could get a flyswatter or newspaper and smash you. You keep trying to get out. You fly to the large glass window by my chair and crawl all around the glass, looking for any way out. I still think I should smash you to the glass with a flyswatter. You can sting me, and that hurts.

You're just trying to get out on your own. You keep crawling on the glass from corner to corner, looking for a way outside. What if I give you a chance? So maybe I'll help you get out. I'll grab you with two fingers by the back of your wings, open the door, and let you go outside. But this could hurt your wings, and maybe you would turn around and sting me with your tail.

I have an idea, Mr. Wasp. I bought some small plastic cups with lids the other day. I'll trap you to the glass with an inverted plastic cup. Then I'll slide the lid between you and the glass to seal the plastic cup, thus trapping you inside the plastic cup. I can open the door to the outside and release you. You might find your house by the garage. I'll give it a try, Mr. Wasp. No promises. Don't sting me with your tail.

It works! Mr. Wasp is free! To my surprise, Mr. Wasp stops as soon as he is back outside. He turns to me and says, "I'll bring you good fortune!"

You never know where your good fortune might come from, so look inside your heart. The source might be right on the kitchen ceiling.

SUK'S MAGIC DRY-CLEANING MACHINE

Suk is my wife's name. She recently bought a dry-cleaning business. It cleans clothes by using a dry-cleaning machine much like a big washing machine cleans clothes. The clothes go in dirty, and when the machine stops, the clothes are clean.

The dry-cleaning business is an old one, and the dry-cleaning machine is very old. Part of the controls on the machine don't work. The automatic control for the automatic run cycle doesn't function properly, so we can't use that control. This makes us clean the clothes by the manual operation control only. We have to know which buttons to push and how many minutes they must run before we push the next button. There are about twenty buttons to push from start to finish. A lot of buttons to push. You have to know when in the cleaning cycle to push the next button. This makes a lot of work for us, but that is the only way the machine will operate. The whole cleaning process takes about forty-five minutes.

When the former owners showed us how to operate the buttons on the dry-cleaning machine, they showed us a green button and told us to "Never, never, never push the green button."

Suk asked, "What will happen if we push the green button?"

The former owner answered, "No one knows. No one has ever pushed the green button before. But never push the green button."

Suk replied, "Okay, we won't ever push the green button!"

We found out after we bought it that the dry-cleaning business is a tough business to make money. We had problems paying all the expenses and employees. We found out later lots of the dry-cleaning businesses face this financial situation.

Suk told me, "Think positive. Look up and pray to God something will happen."

We had run the dry-cleaning business with its dry-cleaning machine for a long while when, all of a sudden, we accidentally pushed the green button. We were scared. What would we do now? The machine kept running and running and running. We couldn't control it by pushing any of the other buttons. It ran nonstop for about three hours. Then things suddenly got quiet, and the dry-cleaning machine stopped. We looked in the glass door of the machine and could see the clothes. The clothes looked okay.

We slowly opened the machine's door, and the clothes still looked okay. We started to take the clothes out of the dry-cleaning machine, slowly at first. We carefully checked to see if anything was wrong. Then we saw money: green paper money. Lots of green paper money. We were scared. What could we do? Where did this money come from? We didn't have any answers. We thought for a while and came up with only one answer. It must have been the green button we accidentally pushed. No one had ever pushed that button before.

After that happened, we thanked God and promised to only push the green button for green paper money in emergencies.

This is the true story about green paper money coming out of an old dry-cleaning machine. Where do you think the green paper money came from?

Thank you, God. We needed the money to keep our dry-cleaning business going.

ELIZABETH WEARS BABY SOCKS

Early in the morning, when Suk and I are getting ready for work at the dry cleaners, a store we own, Elizabeth wants to go. Elizabeth is our dog. Elizabeth goes down the stairs and waits by the garage door. Suk makes sure Elizabeth eats her breakfast and then gives Elizabeth veterinarian-prescribed medicine for her seizures. When we are finished getting ready to leave for work, we go to the garage door and open it. We go into the garage and turn on the light. We push the garage door button, which makes the electric garage door open. Suk gets in the car on the passenger side, ready to leave.

I slip my tennis shoes on while sitting in the plastic chair by the garage door. I get up from the chair, open the garage door, and enter the garage. I pull the door to the garage shut behind me. I stop by the stairs and turn off the house lights. Elizabeth starts jumping on the door, and trying to push the door open. I slowly pull the door shut. I stop a few times to tell Elizabeth, who is barking at the top of her voice, "You can't go." Elizabeth keeps barking at the top of her voice. I keep saying, "You can't go, Elizabeth." She keeps barking and jumping up and down on the bottom step.

That is how Elizabeth broke the toenail on her paw, jumping up and down on the bottom stair. All Elizabeth's toenails had grown very long as we forgot to take her to the veterinarian to get her nails cut. We didn't know at the time that Elizabeth broke her toenail. She kept barking all the time when Suk and I left for work.

One day, Suk and I got home from work late, around seven in the evening. There was no Elizabeth to greet us as normal at the garage door when we came into the house. Suk and I called her, but she didn't answer by coming to greet us. We went into the living room and found Elizabeth, lying on the sofa. She didn't want to get up. Suk and I kept calling her to get up and come to us, but Elizabeth wouldn't get up. Suk and I went into the kitchen, and Elizabeth finally got up. She was holding one paw up and barely walking on the other three paws. We called her name again, and Elizabeth wobbled up the stairs to the kitchen on three paws, holding up the other paw.

I picked up Elizabeth and looked at the paw she had been holding up. I couldn't see anything wrong. I moved her toenails. One was broken but still hanging on. She must have broken her toenail that morning while jumping on the bottom step by the garage door.

I called the veterinarian, who said to bring Elizabeth to be examined. We took her in that afternoon. The doctor said Elizabeth would have to stay at the doctor's office overnight. He would sedate Elizabeth and operate on her toenail. I said okay and left Elizabeth with the doctor.

The next day, the doctor called and said Elizabeth could come home. The doctor had cut the toenail completely out of Elizabeth's paw. The veterinarian said it would grow back.

When the doctor brought Elizabeth out for Suk and I, there was a bandage on her front paw. The doctor said for Suk and I to change the bandage on Elizabeth's paw in twenty-four hours. We were to put a baby sock on Elizabeth's paw, held on by tape. The doctor said the sock would keep Elizabeth from licking her foot.

So Elizabeth wore baby socks for about two weeks, until her foot healed. Elizabeth wears baby socks. What a dog story!

ABOUT THE AUTHOR

The author was born in 1951 in Kansas City, Missouri. He was in the marine reserves a short time but left early due to trouble at home. He graduated from Missouri Western University with a degree in engineering technology. He is presently retired.

ABOUT THE BOOK

This book comes from five true stories, with some added fiction in the story about the wasp on the ceiling and the one about Suk's magic dry-cleaning machine. I hope these stories are unique and entertaining.

Printed in the United States
By Bookmasters